-FOODS OF-
CHINA

by Christine Velure Roholt

BELLWETHER MEDIA • MINNEAPOLIS, MN

Library of Congress Cataloging-in-Publication Data

VeLure Roholt, Christine, author.
 Foods of China / by Christine VeLure Roholt.
    pages cm. -- (Express. Cook with Me)
 Summary: "Information accompanies step-by-step instructions on how to cook Chinese food. The
text level and subject matter are intended for students in grades 3 through 7"-- Provided by publisher.
 Audience: Age 7-12.
 Audience: Grades 3-7.
 Includes bibliographical references and index.
 ISBN 978-1-62617-116-9 (hardcover : alk. paper)
1. Cooking, Chinese--Juvenile literature. 2. Food habits--China--Juvenile literature. 3. China--Social life
and customs--Juvenile literature. I. Title.
 TX724.5.C5V45 2014
 641.5951--dc23
                    2014014020

This edition first published in 2015 by Bellwether Media, Inc.

Printed in the United States of America, North Mankato, MN.

Table of Contents

Cooking the Chinese Way

Like many Asian cultures, the Chinese people value **balance**. They use the concept of **yin and yang** to create this **harmony** in their lives. This involves pairing opposite things that **complement** each other. At mealtime, this means hot and cold, sweet and sour, and soft and crunchy foods are combined.

Like yin and yang, the number five represents balance for the Chinese people. This is why their **cuisine** features five main flavors: sweet, spicy, salty, sour, and bitter. The first two flavors are considered yin and the other three are yang. Chinese cooks are careful to mix ingredients in the best way to create balanced dishes.

Yin Versus Yang

Yin means "dark side of a hill," and yang means "sunny side of a hill."

Eating the Chinese Way

The dinner table is a gathering place for multiple **generations** in China. In a typical household, children, parents, and grandparents all live together under one roof. Mealtime is family time, so dishes are prepared for sharing. To show respect, young people let **elders** eat first. They also reserve seats of honor at the table for them.

The Right Utensil

Chopsticks are used to eat Chinese food. It is never okay to use chopsticks to stab food or poke people.

Rice has been a **staple** food at Chinese dinner tables for thousands of years. Most Chinese dishes are served with the grain. Often, the word *rice* is used in place of the word *food*. This is because the Chinese word for rice, *fan*, also means "meal."

Regional Foods

Across the country, Chinese people have different food preferences. Those in the northern region eat more noodles than those in the southern region, for example. Many **traditional** Chinese dishes are prepared in a variety of ways to feature these regional favorites.

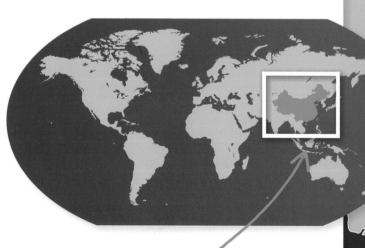

Where is China?

Chengdu

suan la tang:
Hot-and-sour soup with lily buds, edible mushrooms, and bamboo shoots

Shanghai

dazha xie:
Steamed Chinese mitten crabs, also called hairy crabs

Beijing

Beijing kao ya:
Roasted Peking duck with hoisin sauce

Guangzhou

kao ru zhu:
Roasted suckling pig with a sweet-and-sour plum sauce

Tea and Treats

Tea is the beverage enjoyed most often by Chinese people. The drink originated in the country and then spread to Japan and later the rest of the world. In China, tea is an everyday drink. It is also offered as a **gesture**. A cup of tea given to an elder shows respect. A cup of tea can also say, "I'm sorry," or express gratefulness.

Favorite Sips

Dragon Well tea and other green teas are the most popular kinds in China.

Sweets are served with tea, but they are uncommon after meals. If anything follows a meal, it is fresh fruit. The few sweets that are enjoyed are not very sugary. Ingredients like sweet bean paste and sweet agar jellies are used instead.

Getting Ready to Cook

Before you begin cooking, read these safety reminders. Make sure you also read the recipes you will follow. You will want to gather all the ingredients and cooking tools right away.

Safety Reminders

 Ask an adult for permission to start cooking. An adult should be near when you use kitchen appliances or a sharp knife.

 Wash your hands with soapy water before you start cooking. Wash your hands again if you lick your fingers or handle raw meat.

 If you have long hair, tie it back. Remove any bracelets or rings that you have on.

 Wear an apron when you cook. It will protect food from dirt and your clothes from spills and splatters.

 Always use oven mitts when handling hot cookware. If you accidentally burn yourself, run the burned area under cold water and tell an adult.

 If a fire starts, call an adult immediately. Never throw water on a fire. Baking soda can smother small flames. A lid can put out a fire in a pot or pan. If flames are large and leaping, call 911 and leave the house.

 Clean up the kitchen when you are done cooking. Make sure all appliances are turned off.

Jiaozi
gee-OW-za

Chinese Dumplings
Serves 4

Jiaozi are a popular treat that have been around for thousands of years. Because they represent good fortune, they are often eaten during the Chinese New Year.

What You'll Need

- 2 cups Napa cabbage
- 2 green onions
- 2 garlic cloves
- 1 tablespoon ginger
- 1/2 pound ground pork (substitute: ground beef)
- 1 tablespoon rice wine
- 2 tablespoons sesame oil (substitute: olive oil)
- 2 tablespoons soy sauce
- 1 tablespoon cornstarch
- 40 round dumpling wrappers
- olive oil
- 1/2 cup chicken stock (substitute: water)
- large bowl
- large frying pan

Let's Make It!

1

Finely chop the cabbage, onions, garlic, and ginger. Combine in a large bowl with the pork, then mix well.

2

Stir in the rice wine, sesame oil, soy sauce, and cornstarch.

3

Hold 1 dumpling wrapper, then place about 1 teaspoon of the mixture in the middle of the wrapper.

4

Fold the wrapper in half, then pinch the edges together until it is completely sealed.

5

Set the dumplings aside with the edges facing up, then repeat until you run out of the mixture.

6

Add olive oil to a large frying pan and place on medium-high heat. Place the dumplings on the pan with their flat sides down, then cook until the bottoms are brown.

Enjoy!

Add enough chicken stock to cover the bottom of the pan. Cover and cook for about 5 minutes. Serve hot.

Dipping Sauce

Make a dipping sauce for your jiaozi by combining the following ingredients:

- 1/3 cup soy sauce
- 1/3 cup rice wine
- 1 teaspoon sesame oil
- 1/3 cup chopped green onions (optional)

Chá Yè Dàn

cha yee don

Chinese Tea Eggs
Serves 4

Chá yè dàn are a favorite snack sold by Chinese street **vendors** and convenience stores. The cracks in the shells allow the tea to give the eggs beautiful designs and a sweet and **savory** flavor.

What You'll Need

- 6 eggs
- water
- 2 black tea bags
- 1 tablespoon five spice powder
- 2 cinnamon sticks
- 1 teaspoon sugar
- 1/2 teaspoon salt
- 1/2 cup soy sauce
- medium saucepan
- spoon
- large bowl
- plastic wrap

Let's Make It!

1

Place the eggs in a saucepan and cover with water. Bring the water to a boil, then reduce to a simmer. Cook for 7 minutes.

2

Use a spoon to gently move the eggs to a large bowl. Rinse the eggs with cold water until they are cool to the touch.

3

Tap the spoon gently against the eggs to make even cracks throughout the shells. Then place the eggs in an empty saucepan.

4

Add the tea bags, five spice powder, cinnamon sticks, sugar, salt, and soy sauce. If needed, add water to fully cover the eggs, then heat to a simmer for 30 minutes.

5

Transfer the eggs and tea to a large bowl. Cover and let sit for at least 3 hours.

Enjoy!

Lucky Eggs

Tea eggs are also traditionally eaten during the Chinese New Year. They are said to represent growth and wealth.

Peel the shells off of the eggs, then serve warm or cold.

17

Pai Huang Gua

pie hwong gwa

Chinese Smashed Cucumbers
Serves 4

Pai huang gua is commonly served as an appetizer at Chinese restaurants. This light and refreshing salad pairs perfectly with most main dishes.

What You'll Need

- 2 cucumbers
- 1 smashed garlic clove
- 1 teaspoon soy sauce
- 1 teaspoon rice vinegar
- 3 teaspoons sugar
- 1/2 teaspoon sesame oil
- 1/4 teaspoon red pepper flakes
- knife
- bowl
- plastic wrap

Let's Make It!

1

Use a knife to cut off the ends of each cucumber, then cut the length of each cucumber in half. Cut these in half again so that each cucumber is now in 4 long pieces.

2

Chop these pieces into bite-sized slices.

3

Using the side of the knife, carefully press on the slices. The pieces should be slightly mashed.

4

In a bowl, combine the smashed garlic, soy sauce, vinegar, sugar, and sesame oil, then add the cucumber slices.

5

Cover the bowl with plastic wrap, then let the cucumbers marinate in the refrigerator for at least 30 minutes. Sprinkle on the red pepper flakes, then serve cold.

Cooking Tip!

For a stronger flavor, marinate the cucumbers longer.

Smash It Up!

Smashing the cucumbers with the side of the knife softens the edges of the slices. This helps the cucumbers absorb more of the marinade flavors.

Enjoy!

Yi Mein

yee main

Chinese Longevity Noodles
Serves 4

Yi mein is a popular dish traditionally served during birthday celebrations and the Chinese New Year. The length of the noodles represents living a long and healthy life.

What You'll Need

- 12 ounces yi mein noodles
- 3/4 pound diced chicken
- 1 teaspoon cornstarch
- 1/2 teaspoon salt
- 1/8 teaspoon white pepper
- 2 tablespoons olive oil
- 1 minced garlic clove
- 1 pinch red pepper flakes (optional)

- 2 cups vegetables (recommended: sliced mushrooms, red pepper, snow peas, bean sprouts, chopped cabbage)
- 1/2 cup chopped green onion (optional)
- medium saucepan
- strainer
- bowl
- large frying pan

Let's Make It!

1

Add water to a medium saucepan, then bring to a boil over high heat. Add the yi mein noodles, then cook until tender.

2

Transfer the noodles to a strainer, then rinse with cold water.

3

Add the cornstarch, salt, and pepper to a bowl. Toss the chicken pieces in the mixture, then refrigerate the chicken for 10 minutes.

4

Combine 1 tablespoon of olive oil, garlic, and red pepper flakes in a large frying pan over medium-high heat. Add the chicken pieces, then stir-fry until chicken is fully cooked.

5

Add 1 tablespoon of olive oil and the vegetables to the frying pan, then stir-fry for 2 minutes.

Make the Sauce

To make the sauce, combine the following ingredients:

- 1/4 cup soy sauce
- 1 teaspoon oyster sauce
- 1 teaspoon sesame oil
- 1/4 teaspoon white pepper
- 1/8 teaspoon sugar

Enjoy!

Add the sauce to the pan, then stir-fry for 2 minutes. Remove from heat and mix in the noodles, then top with the chopped green onions.

To a Long Life

Chinese people try not to break *yi mein* noodles as they eat. They want to keep the noodles long to represent a long life.

Glossary

balance—an equal or proportional amount of parts or ingredients

complement—to make something better

cuisine—a style of cooking unique to a certain area or group of people

elders—people of a greater age

generations—groups of family members that have a wide range of ages

gesture—an action to show feelings

harmony—peace or balance

savory—something that tastes salty or spicy

staple—a food that is widely and regularly used

traditional—related to the stories, beliefs, or ways of life that families or groups hand down from one generation to another

vendors—people who sell goods

yin and yang—two principles of Chinese culture that represent darkness and light; yin and yang complement each other.

To Learn More

AT THE LIBRARY

Hankin, Rosemary. *A Chinese Cookbook for Kids*. New York, N.Y.: PowerKids Press, 2014.

Rau, Dana Meachen. *Recipes from China*. Chicago, Ill.: Capstone Raintree, 2014.

Simmons, Walter. *China*. Minneapolis, Minn.: Bellwether Media, 2011.

ON THE WEB

Learning more about China is as easy as 1, 2, 3.

1. Go to www.factsurfer.com.

2. Enter "China" into the search box.

3. Click the "Surf" button and you will see a list of related web sites.

With factsurfer.com, finding more information is just a click away.

Index